Cries From A Humbled Spirit:

An Anthology of Poems Penned to Inspire

SPECIAL EDITION

Keisha Gill-Jacob, Ph.D.

Kingdom Builders Publications LLC

Cries From a Humbled Spirit:
An Anthology of Poems Penned to Inspire
Copyright © 2016 by Keisha Gill-Jacob, Ph.D.
Kingdom Builders Publications

SPECIAL EDITION

All rights reserved. No part of this book may be reproduced or transmitted in any form or by any means without written permission from the author.

ISBN 13: 978-0-692-73350-9
Printed in USA
Go to our website: www.kingdombuilderspublications.com

Photographers
Charles Jacob
Ronald Curry
Book Cover Designs
LoMar Designs

Cries From A Humble Spirit:

This Book Belongs to

DEDICATION

This book is dedicated to
My mother,
Annie Louise Gill

Now I lay me down to sleep,

I pray the Lord my soul to keep.

If I should die before I wake,

I pray the Lord my soul to take.

God bless Mommy, Daddy, Keisha, Anthony, and Eunice.

This prayer is etched in my memory.

Weeksville Projects is where my story began; 1650 Pacific Street, Apt 3C Brooklyn, New York 11213. Every night at 9:00 pm, like clockwork, my mother would kneel beside me, and we would bury our faces in our hands and recite this prayer. Afterward, we would say "Amen" and end the night with a hug and a kiss. Then we'd say, "I love you." Before she left my room, Mom would say, "Good night, sleep tight, don't let the bed bugs bite." It's these memories that keep me centered, grounded, and humble. It is only through the Grace of God that I am alive to share my testimony through the spoken word. This is my life, my testimony on paper. Experiences have put me through several tests; humility and the love of God have given me a testimony. This book is dedicated to my lovely Mother Annie L. Gill. I pray that this anthology of poems blesses someone.

Dear Mom,

Growing up in Weeksville was a great experience for the most part. I can honestly, say that I had an awesome childhood. It was here that I met my closest friends at the tender age of 4, and those women still play an integral role in my life. Weeksville embodied a community of kids and adults who genuinely loved and cared about the wellbeing of others. If we were poor, we did not know because our bond gave us the confidence to hold our heads up and persevere regardless of the circumstances. Motherhood came early for me. To be exact, I was only eighteen. Thank God I was raised to have a thick skin because the naysayers truly raised the stakes. They professed that I would never do anything with my life and other disparaging comments that could have had a negative impact on my self-esteem. However, I knew that I was better than that; I knew that they were wrong, and I knew that God would help me through. Life was even better now that I had this beautiful baby girl and a great support system. Until that awful, heartbreaking phone call I received that would change my life forever. That call that rolls the tape as I type this and today reminds me where my strength comes from.

March 7, 1990 was the hardest day of my life. Do you remember... the day I received the call that Allen and Steven were brutally murdered? Allen was my first love, my daughter's father, and Steven was his brother. I don't want to relive that day – which was the longest of my life – but through my uncontrollable cries, I could hear you saying repeatedly, "Ask God to give you strength," and so I did. I was only 18, but this was the lowest point of my life. The truth is, this experience shackled my thoughts, decisions, and emotions for a very long time. Most people didn't know, including you, but God knows all.

I publicly thank you for loving me unconditionally. I thank you for loving me for who I am even when I let you down. I thank you for being my conduit to Christ. But most of all I thank you for being the glue that held me together when my bottom fell out. Yes, Mother, God gave me strength. He also blessed Mommy, Daddy, Keisha, Anthony, and Eunice just like I asked. He has never let me down and has answered my every prayer. Thank you, Lord for your divine intervention. I believe!

TABLE OF CONTENTS

Dedication	iv
Forward	viii
Mother	9
Teenage Pregnancy	10
A Promise to my Daughters	11
Sisters	12
Brother	13
Family	14
Friends	15
Confronting Mr. Darkness	16
What is a Dad	17
From Us to Dad	18
I wish I Could Call Tyrone	19
D A D	21
My Bypass	22
Circumcision	23
Transparent	24
Random Thoughts	25
Beautifully and Wonderfully Made	26
Imperfections Prayer	27
Faith	28
A Spoken Word	29

Cries From A Humble Spirit:

Trust In The Lord	30
Testimony	31
Baptism	32
Pilot	33
Communication	34
Questions	35
Original	36
Words	37
Resume	37
Moving	38
Wisdom	38
Teachers	38
Trials	39
Caution	39
Help	39
The Gift	40
Masterpiece	41
Inspire	41
Equally Yoked	42
About the Author	43

FOREWORD

Heavenly Father, I thank You for it all. I thank You for the good; I thank You for the not so good. I thank you for the sunshine, and I thank You for the storm. Most of all, I thank You for loving me despite my imperfections. You are the author of my script. In Jesus name I pray. Amen.

When He maketh inquisition for blood, He remembereth them: He forgetteth not the cry of the humble.
KJV Psalm 9-12.

When God created mothers,
He designed you with me in mind.
He knew exactly what I needed—
Even down to the most intricate details—
To get through the most challenging times,
To bend with the wind during the storm,
And to stand stronger when it's over.
I praise him for entrusting me to you
My mother, My mom, My friend.
My unique gift from the Almighty King!

Teenage Pregnancy

Take a good look at me, Miss Teenage Pregnancy…
Yeah, that's who I am… Holding my head high?
Yes, one day I am…
How did I get here? Not much did it take
Leave it to the judgers; it was all a big mistake.
My life is over, just another statistic
But God is my judge and he helped me to see
The sin is in the sex and not the baby.
So my testimony is real; it's profound, and it's true
I tell my testimony in hopes to help you…
So take a good look at me…Ms. Ph.D.
Whoever thought it could actually be me?
But God had a plan, and He knew I would make it
Even during times, I thought I couldn't take it…
Now don't get me wrong, I'm not a proponent of
Teenage pregnancy.
I just want to encourage
He can do for you what he has done for Me!
So take one last look at me.
Miss Teenage Pregnancy, Ms. Ph.D.
And title me a child of the King
Because that's who I really be!

A Promise to My Daughters

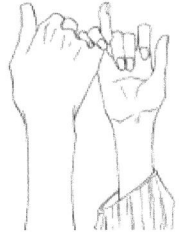

When I think about the goodness of God,

Nothing can compare—

How he strategically placed you in my life

At a time of much despair.

And no matter what the people said,

A smile I chose to wear.

For you gave me hope

And saved my life

When I thought no one cared.

So as I said,

When you were kids,

It was us against the world.

And regardless of what life

Might throw our way

I will always be there for my baby girls!

Sisters

She cried for me.

She didn't even know the depth

Of my situation, but…

She cried for me.

And for every delicate tear drop,

God presented a bottle for her to fill,

Reserved for her low place.

And when her valley experience manifested,

She reached for her bottle of tears

To anoint herself

But decided to give her tears to me.

Her Tears, Her Ministry, My Sister.

Brother

The relationship between a brother and his sisters is one that should be sustained
Throughout a lifetime.
My brother has talked me through some difficult times
If fact, he was the one to tell me through my illness,
"Keisha, you are okay right now."
That one sentence helped me to appreciate the moment
And to be grateful through my trials
I thank God for giving me one brother
And understanding that he would be all I need.
Brother, I write this poem
With the hopes that you understand
That I am listening
Even when you think I'm not.
I'm am a survivor and so are you!

Family

An expression used to describe
A bond so thick
It cannot be broken;
A phrase that embraces imperfections
Along with a perfected effort
To shield one another from harm
And share the experiences of life.
Fam (ILY)
Because ILY is a simple reminder that I Love
You,
Unconditionally,
Family,
You are a present from God,
Crafted by his divine excellence.

There is nothing I revere more than a true friend

in every sense of the word.

Friends understand that the relationship must be reciprocal.

They protect you in your absence

And shield you in your presence.

They continuously make deposits into humanity

Without expecting much in return.

They are not martyrs;

They are God's gift of extended family that is there

Through every hour, without reason

And without question.

That the job is for a lifetime.

Thank God for my friends

Confronting Mr. Darkness

You've claimed many that I love.

I can only pray that their spirits are resting

 Peacefully above

My dad, my granny, Tyrone, my first love

And more…

His brother, my friends, my Aunts, and others I adore

Unfortunately, when you knocked,

There was no place to hide.

It killed a fraction of my spirit when these people died,

Shedding a cold lonely darkness

To the fear I once held inside.

But God shined his light

When the burden was too much to bear.

Now I fear no Evil when the shadow of death is near!

WHAT IS A DAD?

There is an old adage that states
Anyone can be a father,
But it takes a lot to be a dad.
A DAD is someone who cares for your basic needs.
A DAD is someone who protects you from harm.
A DAD is someone who upholds his family with pride.
A DAD is someone who disciplines with love.
A DAD is someone who wipes away your tears.
A DAD is someone who encourages you to keep your head up.
A DAD is someone who cheers for his son at a basketball game.
A DAD is someone who kisses his little girl's knee.
Hoping to take away the pain.
Our DAD was all of these things and more.
Our DAD was a fighter.
Our DAD was a healer.
Our DAD was a leader.
Our DAD was a proud DAD.
Our DAD was Leroy Gill

From us to Dad

Dad, you always listened when no one else would.

You always fought,

even when the battle was too much to bear.

And even though they don't make DADS like you anymore,

we are proud to say that you are our DAD.

We will love you always

and will continue to make you proud

by living in accordance with the principles

that you and MOM have instilled in us.

You have done your job.

Now it is time for you to rest.

Saying goodbye seems too final,

so we will close this by saying:

until we meet at the crossroads.

I Wish I Could Call Tyrone

Erykah Badu has a song that says, "You better call Tyrone".
I wish I could.
Honestly, it would help me understand why you had to leave us so soon.
You were always there for us.
Now there's an empty void
That will never be filled
Despite the fact that I tried to block you out.
The day I came home from my brain surgery
You were right there.
You mentioned that you were going in for back surgery.
You looked me in the eye and said, "You know I could die."
Instead of praying with you,
I asked you not to speak like that.
You listened as I assured you everything was going to be all right.
I'm sorry that I lied to you;

I only wanted to be there
For you the way you were there for me.
The pain cuts deep.
I've asked God to ease the pain;
I've asked God to wrap His arms around those who
were left behind.
If only I could call you,
I would do things much differently.
I love you brother, with every fiber of my being
As I piece together the memories we built.
Rest easy, my brother,
As we all try to carry on with this new normal that
We still have trouble understanding

DAD

Dear angel,
I feel your presence
on your way back to Heaven
Can you deliver a message to my dad?
The first man
to kiss me on the cheek;
the first man to tell me he loves me,
to laugh at my jokes,
to care for my wounds.
The one who believed
I could do anything
but didn't live long enough
in the physical world to see it happen.
Dear angel, can you tell him
if only he was here to wipe away my tears and shield
me from harm,
if only I had five more minutes with him,
I would kiss him on the cheek,
tell him I love him,
laugh at his jokes…
because he is my hero.

MY BYPASS

My heart,
broken into two pieces.
Step back and
take a closer look inside.
Yes, that is you.
If you would do me a favor—
Gently put those two halves together
so I can be whole again

CIRCUMCISION

Dear God,
I come to you as humble as I know how.
I ask that you restore my faith in those in whom I have lost trust.
Father, I ask that you circumcise my heart immediately.
Remove the years of baggage camouflaged as plaque,
Plaque that has hardened and attached itself to my walls in hopes of covering up my hurt and pain.
Dear God, hear my humble cry.
My heartbeat is dull and out of sync with you.
Clean my valves and prevent this coronary.

I need a heart that forgives, and a mind that is totally focused on you.
I plead the blood on any situation that corrupts my thoughts and my ♡ heart;
I plead the blood on anything that is not like the image of You.
Only you can do it, Father
Only you can do it.

In Jesus name I pray for expedient healing
And for healthy Christian living.
Amen

TRANSPARENT

He didn't realize my worth was far more than rubies.

He didn't appreciate my value added.

He just didn't know who I was or even cared about

Who and what I could be.

He left me emotionally stranded for his own selfish gain.

He didn't honor me as a Lady of Light…The Lady Elect

But all the while, God was rocking another to sleep.

Unexpectedly to me, I was given his rib

I became the WO to his MAN…His Wo-Man, his Wife,

His friend for Life.

His carnal man loves me, but his spiritual man protects.

And with his Godly actions

He apologized for the hurt and pain others may have caused

With no exception to his carnal man.

RANDOM THOUGHTS

Can some of the holy and sanctified

still hear a word from the

"Little people?"

If we only took the time to talk to people, we would be

surprised to know

where the Creator walked

to bring them out of their situation.

I was one...

So I know Jesus visits the clubs,

the projects, and so on.

Now I ask,

are you seeking religion or a relationship?

My point?

Stop judging people because

you are also a work in progress.

I am so glad God forgives.

Beautiful and Wonderfully Made

I pray that the person reading this prayer

will benefit from my life,

that I can encourage others

to be still when necessary

and attain the strength to not only face,

but survive the unexpected.

I pray that the person reading this message

will recognize their self-worth

because we all have a purpose.

You are beautiful and wonderfully made.

AMEN

Imperfections PRAYER

Though drugs and alcohol may not be my vice,

money and power may not be my type,

Dear Lord, clear my vision

And allow me to see…

The deep

imperfections

Embedded in me.

Amen

Faith

I walk by faith and not by sight.

My soul is in trouble…So I try to live right.

Sometimes I'm conflicted, so I slip and I fall.

If only I could avoid so many brick walls!

I searched for a window to mentally end life and jump.

Just as I leaped, God avoided the thump.

He didn't want my blood but covered me in His instead

And refused to let me harm a hair on my head.

He reached out his Arms and invited me in.

I advise you to try him; he's my trusted Friend.

Now I walk by faith, not by sight.

Time is running out, people

And I'm determined

To get this right!

A Spoken Word

You counted me out,
But I wasn't done,
So I sent a prayer to my Father
Through his only begotten Son.
And what do you know, he actually replied:
"I am the Omnipresent Truth
That your dreams will never die.
Now this… I have proven.
"Remember the stripes on my back?
Now keep pressing forward
And don't you turn back.
Just walk in my light;
It shall keep you on track."

Trust In the Lord

I am the Father,

The Lord Jesus Christ

Hold on to me with all of your might.

I am the one Who has set you free.

Those who believe are free indeed.

I am the Alpha, the Omega too;

From beginning to end I will see you through.

Keep spreading the gospel and live what you speak

For my undying love, I'll never retreat.

I am the Father,

The Lord Jesus Christ.

Hold on to Me with all of your might.

I am the one who has set you free.

Those who believe are free indeed!

Testimony

I've been through enough in this lifetime

to know that everything works together for your **GOoD!**

My test is for me, but my testimonies are for you.

I have never been pretentious and will never be.

I am just Keisha, nothing magical,

A child of the King!

It doesn't matter what people say or think about you.

Whatever it is, it's going to be all right.

Hope this helps someone... Now, bless someone today.

Baptism

It wasn't long after the baptism

that I realized I left some things

down in the water.

Renewed, refreshed, restart!

Pilot

God is my pilot

And my GPS.

He carries me on His Wings;

Therefore, I'm never lost.

Communication

He listens when no one else does.

I know this is true

Because he answers my every prayer.

He is not just

A telepathic friend that permits my

Prayers to wander aimlessly in space.

He listens when no one else does.

I know this is true

Because the impression of his footprints

Are still in my heart

From all my answered prayers.

Blessed be the matchless name of the Lord.

Questions

Who do you think you are?
And why are you here?
How is it wherever I turn,
You are always there?
Why are you the cause of my sorrow and tears?
And how do you know
When happiness is near?
Why do you shackle my self-confidence,
Injecting your thoughts of fear?
And bottleneck my dreams
By screaming lies LOUDLY in my ears?
Well, as of today, you hear me
And hear me loud and clear
Brain tumor, find another home
Because your lease is up here!

ORIGINAL

My skin is dark and *beautiful*.

My hair is kinky yet beautiful.

My radiant smile is BEAUTIFUL.

My cheek bones are high yet BEAUTIFUL.

My hips are wide yet *beautiful*.

Because God made me in His **beautiful** image.

I am an original;

There is no other like me.

I am *beautiful* just the way I am.

No carbon copies;

Strictly **ORIGINAL**.

WORDS

FRAGILE!

Please handle with caution.

If misused, we may hurt, cut or cause deep wounds.

WORDS!

RESUME

Ladies, stop complaining about your man

if you gave him the job

without reviewing his resume.

Moving

THE DEVIL IS SNIPPING AT MY HEELS, SO

I KNOW I'M MOVING IN THE RIGHT DIRECTION.

WISDOM

A *little* **WISDOM**:

Don't knock someone off their feet because you finally got on yours.

TEACHERS

Education is the lock to success,
But an exemplary teacher
Is the one who holds the key

Trials

So I've learned,
Throughout every experience…
to hold my head down only when I pray!

Caution

People will use you

Until they have no use for you.

Help

Help someone along the way;

It's never about you.

The Gift

God gave me this gift

Which looked very different.

It wasn't in a big box or wrapped in a bow.

Still, it took me some time to unwrap it.

At first, I didn't even recognize how special it was

Or how it would change my life…

Or even the life of others.

Teaching… That is my gift, my ministry.

What is your gift?

Masterpiece

"Teachers are the potter,
Students are the clay...
Are you proud of your masterpiece?"

INSPIRE

Teach the kids you have

Not the kids you desire

"Believe in your students.

Inspire them to reach beyond.

One day they will pay it forward!"

Equally Yoked

There is no magical potion.
The signs are clear, and we must not ignore them.
The key is to choose a mate who is
Equally strong and secure within himself.
With an independent woman by his side
This type of man excels
Because he understands that a strong woman
Walks beside and not behind him.
He doesn't constantly compete with her,
Yet, he holds her hand
As she gives birth to her dreams.
He is the pulse to her aspirations.
Because they put God first,
They make their union divorce proof.
Together the two are unstoppable,
Empowered because they are Equally Yoked
And believe God's promise
Stated in Proverbs 18:22.
"He who finds a wife finds a good thing."

ABOUT THE AUTHOR

Dr. Keisha Gill-Jacob – 1971, a New York native, is a wife, mother, author, poet, educator, and entrepreneur. Her fondest and most devastating moments all stem from her childhood home in Weeksville, Gardens projects. She attributes a great deal of her life's inspiration to the experiences she's shared with her childhood friends, much of which have inspired her to author her own book. Dr. Gill-Jacob knew that God would take her on a path that would mature her into an individual that would serve as a role model for others.

Dr. Gill-Jacob is the CEO and Founder of IMBUED, LLC. Her business strives to promote wellness in its totality by bringing no gimmick premium products to the market since 2014.

Dr. Gill-Jacob continues her lifelong passion of educating the youth. She has dedicated her services to students with special needs for 25 years. She has brought change in various educational settings and her experience ranges from paraprofessional, teacher, local support teacher, assistant principal, and an executive director of turnaround schools. She currently serves as the Director of High School Education at the Bancroft School. Keisha has worked in New York City Public Schools, New Jersey, Maryland Public Schools, and the District of Columbia Public Schools. Dr. Gill-Jacob earned her Bachelor's degree in Psychology from the College of New Rochelle, Master's degree in Special Education with a dual certification in Emotional/Learning Disabilities from Long Island University, and her Doctorate degree in Educational Leadership K-12 from Capella University. She is a testament to women who aspire to inspire. Currently residing in Maryland with her husband Charles and five children; Alakeisha, Tykwon, Tiffany, Sonovia, Lauren, and one grandson Connor that keeps her on her feet. She is a proud member of Sigma Gamma Rho Sorority Incorporated and wholeheartedly believes in "Greater Service, Greater Progress."

www.ingramcontent.com/pod-product-compliance
Lightning Source LLC
Chambersburg PA
CBHW061816290426
44110CB00026B/2888